ALL ABOUT...

THE

GREAT
PLAGUE

PAM ROBSON

Text © Pam Robson 1996
Illustrations © Dez Marwood 1996
Photographs © Sources credited

First published in Great Britain by Macdonald Young Books

Reprinted in 2002 by Hodder Wayland, an imprint of Hodder Children's Books

© Hodder Wayland 1996

Hodder Children's Books, a division of Hodder Headline Ltd,
338 Euston Road, London NW1 3BH

A CIP catalogue for this book is available from the British Library.

ISBN 0 7500 1934 4

Editor: Annie Scothern
Designer: Jane Hannath
Picture credits: Mary Evans Picture Library - 7, 14t, 30, 37r, 38, 39r, 43.
Museum of London - title page, 14b, 26, 27, 31t&b, 34, 35, 37l, 39b. The Bridgeman
Art Library - cover, 9b, 13t, 20, 41. Frank Spooner Pictures - 6. The Mansell Collection -
11. V&A Museum - 12, 40. Yorkshire Museum - 13b. Society of Antiquaries of London -
19. Michale Holford - 28. Science and Society Picture Library - 23, National Maritime
Museum Picture Library - 25. Philadelphia Museum of Art, the Philip S Collins Collection,
given by Mrs Philip S Collins in memory of her husband - 9t. The Times Newspapers
Limited 1994, "European Alert at Airports..." from The Times 28 September 1994,
" Menace of Deadly Old Enemy" from The Times 24 September 1994 - 44

The author and publishers thank the above for permission to reproduce their photographs.

Printed in Hong Kong

Titles in the ALL ABOUT... series:
THE FIRST WORLD WAR
THE GREAT FIRE OF LONDON
THE GREAT PLAGUE
THE SECOND WORLD WAR
THE TUDORS
THE VICTORIANS

ALL ABOUT...

THE

GREAT PLAGUE

PAM ROBSON

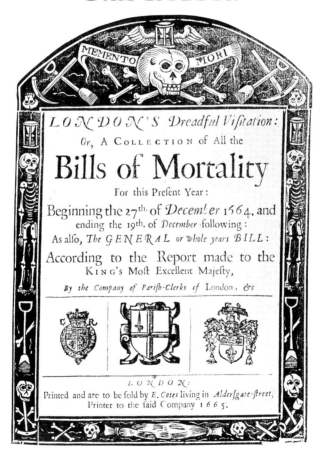

MEMENTO MORI

LONDON'S Dreadful Visitation:

Or, A COLLECTION of All the

Bills of Mortality

For this Present Year:

Beginning the 27th of December 1664, and
ending the 19th of December following:

As also, The GENERAL or whole years BILL:

According to the Report made to the
KING's Most Excellent Majesty,

By the Company of Parish-Clerks of London, &c

LONDON:
Printed and are to be sold by E. Cotes living in Aldersgate-street,
Printer to the said Company 1 6 6 5.

HODDER
Wayland

TIMELINE

1345 *Conjunction of the planets Saturn, Jupiter and Mars; reports of catastrophes in the Far East; the Black Death reaches the Black Sea*

1348 *The Black Death reaches south-west England*

1349 *Mass burials at Tournai in Belgium*

1603-12 *Plague recurs every year in London*

1625 *Plague in London; public health regulations are issued*

1628 *William Harvey discovers that the blood circulates around the body*

1660 *Charles II returns to England as king; granting of a charter to the Royal Society; Samuel Pepys begins to keep his diaries*

1664 *First sighting of a comet in December*

1665

March *War is declared between England and Holland; second sighting of a comet over London*

April *First known victim of the Great Plague dies*

May *Plague deaths causing unease in London*

August *London's streets are empty*

September *The Great Plague reaches its peak in London; outbreak of plague in Eyam, Derbyshire*

1666

February *Charles II returns to London*

September *The Great Fire of London*

1669 *Pepys stops writing his diaries*

1894 *Discovery of bacillus* Yersinia Pestis

1994 *Suspected outbreak of plague in India*

CONTENTS

THE PLAGUE IS BACK!

"**B**ubonic plague makes deadly global comeback." This headline could have been used to describe the plague that swept across Europe 600 years ago, reaching England in 1348. Before this the word 'plague' had meant any infectious disease. The outbreak in 1348 later became known as the Black Death, possibly because of the dark patches that appeared on the bodies of victims. But historians now believe it was bubonic plague. The disease reappeared at regular intervals in England until the next major outbreak – the Great Plague of London in 1665. Plague still recurs in some areas of the world today. In fact the headline above is quite recent, 3 March 1994. It shows how the fear of plague is still with us.

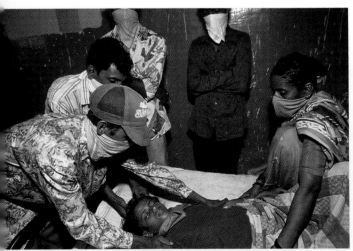

A 20th-century plague victim.

Population figures dropped dramatically in many European countries after the Black Death of 1348. Almost one quarter of the population of Europe died – as many as 25 million people.

This picture vividly expresses the terror experienced by people when plague struck.

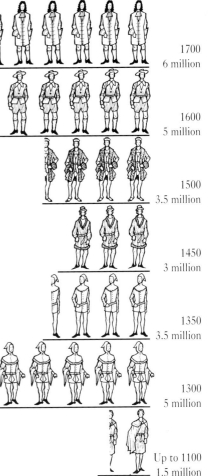

1700
6 million

1600
5 million

1500
3.5 million

1450
3 million

1350
3.5 million

1300
5 million

Up to 1100
1.5 million

COUNTRY	CASES	DEATHS
USA	13	2
Madagascar	198	26
Zaire	390	140
Brazil	25	0
Peru	120	4
China	35	6
Mongolia	12	4
Burma	528	3
Vietnam	437	13

This chart lists the reported cases of plague in nine countries for 1992. The numbers seem small when compared with those for the Black Death.

7

"A VAST RAIN OF FIRE..."

In 1345 news of catastrophes in the Far East, including earthquakes, volcanic eruptions, floods, famine and plague, travelled across the Continent to Britain. These were seen as omens of bad things to come. The population of Europe was increasing. A series of wet, cold summers had ruined harvests. The starving people had little resistance to disease. The Black Death reached the Black Sea in 1345, carried by rats on board trading ships.

The lines show how the Black Death spread from the Far East through ports on the Black Sea and the Mediterranean to Europe. It reached south-west England in the winter of 1348.

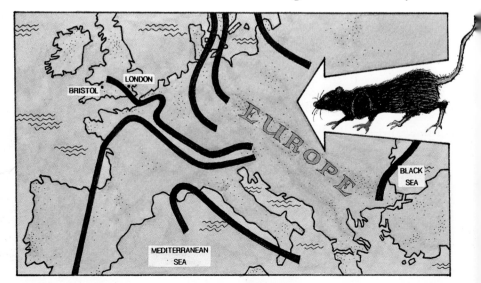

Plague literature is filled with stories of bad signs or omens. Here an earthquake and a 'rain of fire' (volcanic eruption) can be seen.

Italian soldiers fighting the Mongolian army near the Black Sea were said to have been bombarded with plague-ridden bodies. Infected Italian sailors took the plague into French ports. English soldiers fighting in France may have carried the infection back with them, or it may have reached English ports on trading ships.

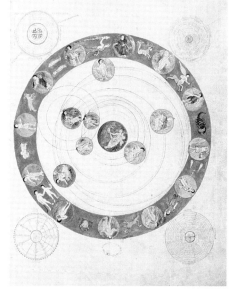

Some people in medieval Europe blamed a conjunction of the planets Saturn, Jupiter and Mars that took place in 1345 for the outbreak of plague.

PLAGUE CARRIERS

I t was not until the end of the 19th century that scientists discovered that plague is spread by bacteria carried by fleas on black rats. Plague can now be cured by treating victims with the antibiotic tetracycline. Bubonic plague affects the lymph glands, which become enlarged and filled with pus. 'Bubo' comes from the Greek word for groin – the area where the first buboes often appear.

Some bacteria are useful, others are harmful. A rod-shaped bacterium is known as a bacillus. The bacillus moves using whip-like flagella.

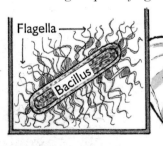

Flagella
Bacillus

Bacillus Yersinia Pestis was identified as the cause of bubonic plague. This bacterium is carried by fleas on black rats. Victims ache, sweat, vomit and cough blood. Diarrhoea and delirium follow and painful, pus-filled swellings (buboes) break out. Death comes after three days.

In the Middle Ages, plague was seen by religious fanatics called flagellants as a punishment from God. To atone for their sins they travelled all over Europe, lashing themselves with iron-tipped whips.

Pneumonic plague affects the lungs and is very infectious because it is spread through coughs and sneezes. But the worst strain is septicaemic plague. This is always fatal because it attacks the bloodstream.

Black rats were finally driven out of Britain by brown rats, which do not carry plague fleas.

11

IMAGES AND CHARMS

A 14th-century dance of death.

The belief that infection came from 'bad air' was accepted for centuries until scientists discovered bacteria and began to understand how disease spreads. Magic charms were frequently worn as protection against disease. After the Black Death of 1348, death became a popular theme in art.

A dog licks the wounds of St. Roch, who is carrying a bell to warn people of his approach.

Mass burials at Tournai in Belgium, 1349.

Danse Macabre was a processional play performed in 14th-century Europe, in which men dressed as skeletons did a dance of death. Images of death appeared in stained-glass windows and on tomb carvings. Plague recurred in Europe in 1360 and 1369, and then every few years until the early 18th century. In Spain St. Roch became the patron saint of the sick, particularly those suffering from plague. Statues from the 16th century often show him as a plague victim himself.

This 15th-century charm, known as the Middleham Jewel, was found in 1984 in north-east England. It was worn as a charm against illness and the magical word 'anazapta' appears on it.

13

"I SAW THE COMET..."

Samuel Pepys was an eyewitness to the Great Plague of London in 1665, and he describes in his famous diary the dreadful events he saw. In London, plague was not unusual so the first deaths attracted little attention.

The Diseases and Casualties this Week.

	Imposthume — 11
	Infants — 16
	Killed by a fall from the Belfrey at Alhallows the Great — 1
	Kingsevil — 2
	Lethargy — 1
	Palsie — 1
	Plague — 7165
Abortive — 5	Rickets — 17
Aged — 43	Rising of the Lights — 11
Ague — 2	Scowring — 5
Apoplexie — 1	Scurvy — 2
Bleeding — 2	Spleen — 1
Burnt in his Bed by a Candle at St. Giles Cripplegate — 1	Spotted Feaver — 101
Canker — 1	Stilborn — 17
Childbed — 42	Stone — 2
Chrisomes — 18	Stopping of the stomach — 9
Consumption — 134	Strangury — 1
Convulsion — 64	Suddenly — 1
Cough — 2	Surfeit — 49
Droptie — 33	Teeth — 121
Feaver — 309	Thrush — 5
Flox and Small-pox — 5	Timpany — 1
Frighted — 3	Tissick — 11
Gowt — 1	Vomiting — 3
Grief — 3	Winde — 3
Griping in the Guts — 51	Wormes — 15
Jaundies — 5	

Christned { Males — 95, Females — 81, In all — 176 } Buried { Males — 4095, Females — 4202, In all — 8297 } Plague — 7165

Increased in the Burials this Week — 607
Parishes clear of the Plague — 4   Parishes Infected — 126

The Assize of Bread set forth by Order of the Lord Maior and Court of Aldermen; A penny Wheaten Loaf to contain Nine Ounces and a half, and three half-penny White Loaves the like weight.

Samuel Pepys wrote his diaries in shorthand from 1660-69.

In March 1665 war broke out between England and Holland. In the same month a comet was seen streaking across the sky. Pepys had recorded sighting a comet three months before.

Each parish in London had to produce a regular Bill of Mortality listing the number of deaths and the causes. Plague was listed in nearly every year. Smallpox, tuberculosis and rickets were also common.

Year	Plague Deaths		Year	Plague Deaths
1603	29,083		1609	4,240
1604	896		1610	1,803
1605	444		1611	627
1606	2,124		1612	64
1607	2,352		1625	41,313
1608	2,352		1665	100,000

Deaths from plague in London, 1603-65.

To the superstitious population, this was very significant. Astrologers expressed concern over the number of people who had died from plague. It was said that God was angry. The first acknowledged victim of the Great Plague was Margaret Ponteous, buried on 12 April 1665 at St. Paul's church in Covent Garden, London. As the epidemic took hold, people looked for scapegoats. Many tried to blame the Catholics.

To the people of London it seemed that God was angry. On 17 December 1664 Pepys wrote: "Mighty talk there is of this comet that is seen a'nights..." On 24 December he wrote: "I saw the comet..."

15

THE STREETS OF LONDON

I n January 1665 the population of London was about 500,000. Over 100,000 people were to die in the coming months from plague. Within the old city walls, a crowded square mile – known then and now as the 'City of London' – stretched along the river. Wooden houses and shops with overhanging upper storeys lined the narrow, rubbish-filled streets. Smoke from coal fires and furnaces polluted the air. Hackney carriages and large wagons rumbled over the cobblestones, while the familiar cries of the raucous street-sellers echoed through the streets.

Horse dung, rotting rubbish and raw sewage created a continuous stink. The filthy London streets were cleaned by 'rakers'. Streams like Bridewell Brook were open sewers. Cesspits had to be emptied at night.

"New river water!" and "Lilly white vinegar, threepence (3d) a quarter!" were familiar cries. Pepys knew many of the street-sellers by name.

The writer Daniel Defoe was only five years old during the Great Plague. When he wrote his memoirs much later, he described how shopkeepers had dipped all coins in vinegar to prevent infection spreading.

17

OUTSIDE THE CITY OF LONDON

I n 1665, areas to the south of London Bridge like Southwark were still villages. To the north, places as close to the City of London as Islington were surrounded by fields. Westwards, the walk to Westminster past St. Paul's Cathedral was a pleasant stroll through gardens. Eastwards, past the Tower of London, the Mile End Road became a country lane. The suburbs to the north of Westminster did not extend beyond what is now Trafalgar Square.

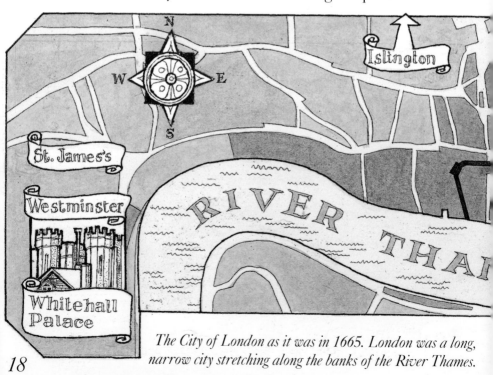

The City of London as it was in 1665. London was a long, narrow city stretching along the banks of the River Thames.

Samuel Pepys watched the Duke of York playing the new game of Pell-mell in St. James's Park in 1661.

St. James's in Westminster was the most fashionable part of London and was favoured by the rich. The king's court was at Whitehall.

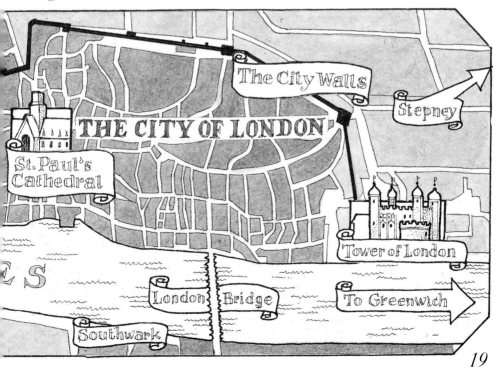

LONDON'S HIGHWAY

In the 1660s there was only one bridge across the River Thames – London Bridge. Houses and shops had been built on it and some were six storeys high. The turret at the southern end of the bridge was sometimes hung with the heads of traitors, which were left there until they rotted. The river was London's highway. Thames watermen rowed their boats, known as wherries, to and fro across the river.

Built in the 13th century, the old London Bridge was the only bridge across the River Thames at the time of the Great Plague.

The heads of traitors were stuck on pikes at the entrance to the old London Bridge as a warning to wrongdoers!

There were regular wherry services from Westminster to Greenwich and water taxis, known as skiffs, for hire. When plague struck London in 1665, many watermen fled with their families. On 20 September Pepys noted: "...what a sad time it is to see no boats on the river." This was the worst week of the Great Plague.

In A Journal of the Plague Year, *written in 1722, Daniel Defoe wrote:*
"I found that the watermen on the river above the bridge found means to convey themselves away up river...their whole families in their boats..."

SAMUEL PEPYS: EYEWITNESS

I n his fascinating diaries Samuel Pepys describes the major events of the 1660s in England, including the Restoration of King Charles II in 1660, the Great Plague of 1665 and the Great Fire of London in 1666. At the age of 15, Pepys had witnessed the execution of Charles I. Oliver Cromwell had become the next ruler of England – he had closed theatres and even turned Christmas into a fasting day!

Pepys' diaries cover a nine-year period. He stopped writing them when he was only 36 years old because he believed he was going blind. He even made tube spectacles from rolled paper to help him see.

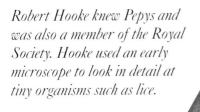

Robert Hooke knew Pepys and was also a member of the Royal Society. Hooke used an early microscope to look in detail at tiny organisms such as lice.

Pepys' wife found lice in her husband's hair. He had little time for personal hygiene – like many others at that time!

After Cromwell's death, Pepys sailed to Holland aboard the *Royal Charles* to bring Charles II back to England. Pepys became Clerk to the Navy Board, earning £350 a year. Later he became a Member of Parliament, and in 1665 he was elected a Fellow of the newly created Royal Society.

In common with a lot of men in Restoration times, Pepys liked to wear fashionable clothes: "I put on my best black cloth suit, trimmed with scarlett ribbon..." He also carried a silver-knobbed walking stick, which can still be seen in the Museum of London.

During the Great Plague Pepys stopped wearing his new wig in case the hair from a dead plague victim had been used to make it.

PEPYS' DIARY OF THE PLAGUE

" **7** JUNE *The hottest day that ever I felt in my life. This day, much against my will, I did in Drury Lane see two or three houses marked with a red cross upon the doors, and 'Lord have mercy upon us' writ there...*

27 JULY *To Hampton Court, where I saw the King and Queene set out towards Salisbury...in all about 1,700 [died] of the plague...*

30 JULY *It was a sad noise to hear our bell to toll and ring so often today; either for death or burials; I think five or six times.*

10 AUGUST *...in great trouble to see the Bill this week rise so high...about 3,000 [died] of the plague.*

12 AUGUST *The people die so, that now it seems they are fain to carry the dead to be buried by day-light, the nights not sufficing to do it in. And my Lord Mayor commands people to be within at nine at night...*

31 AUGUST *...the plague having a great encrease this week...making the general Bill 7,000, odd 100; and the plague above 6,000...our fleet gone out to find the Dutch...*

During the time of the Great Plague, England and Holland were at war.

3 SEPTEMBER
Up, and put on my coloured silk suit, very fine, and my new periwigg, bought a good while since, but darst not wear it because the plague was in Westminster when I bought it. And it is a wonder what will be the fashion after the plague is done as to periwiggs, for nobody will dare to buy any haire for fear of the infection, that it had been cut off the heads of people dead of the plague.

14 SEPTEMBER ...my meeting dead corpses of the plague, carried to be buried close to me at noon-day through the city in Fenchurch Street. To see a person sick of the sores, carried close by me by Gracechurch in a hackney-coach...

27 SEPTEMBER Here I saw this week's Bill of Mortality, wherein, blessed be to God! there is above 1,800 decrease...

31 DECEMBER But now the plague is abated almost to nothing... The Dutch war goes on very ill... **"**

25

THE 'KING'S TOUCH'

King Charles II lived at Whitehall Palace in Westminster, London. He carried out many public duties there, including the ancient ceremony for sufferers from 'king's evil', or scrofula, which caused swellings in the neck. In this religious ritual, the king touched each victim to help cure the disease.

The Manner of His Majesties Curing the Disease, CALLED THE KINGS-EVIL.

Pepys wrote in 1661: "I went to the Banquet-house, and there saw the King heale, the first time that I ever saw him do it..."

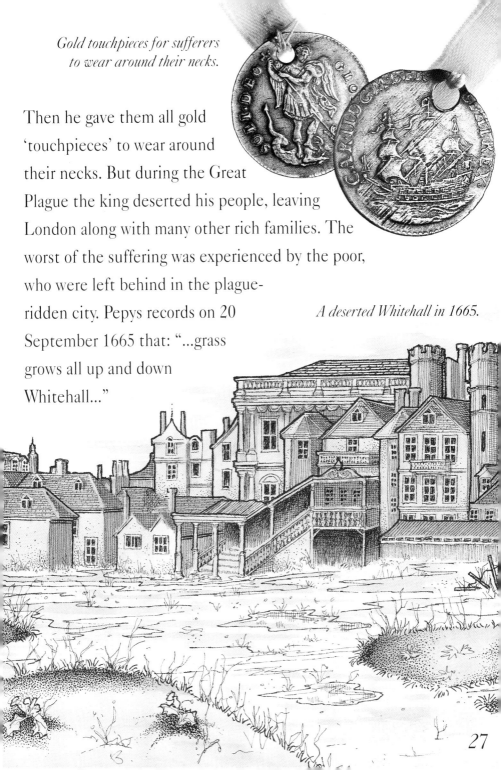

Gold touchpieces for sufferers to wear around their necks.

Then he gave them all gold 'touchpieces' to wear around their necks. But during the Great Plague the king deserted his people, leaving London along with many other rich families. The worst of the suffering was experienced by the poor, who were left behind in the plague-ridden city. Pepys records on 20 September 1665 that: "...grass grows all up and down Whitehall..."

A deserted Whitehall in 1665.

NINE O' CLOCK CURFEW

Charles II had reopened London's theatres on his Restoration in 1660, but during the Great Plague they were closed down again. The first coffee-house opened in London in 1652 and by 1663 there were 82. A dish of coffee cost one penny (1d) and newspapers were provided free. London also had countless inns, ale-houses and taverns.

Pepys wrote in May 1665:
"To the Coffee-house, where all the news is of the Dutch being gone
out and news of the plague growing upon us in this town..."

Orders for health.

Care to be had of unwholfome Fifh or Flefh, and of mufty Corne.

THat fpeciall care be taken, that no ftinking Fifh, or unwholfome Flefh, or muftie Corne, or other corrupt fruits of what fort foever, be fuffered to bee fold about the City or any part of the fame.

That the Brewers and Tipling houfes be looked un-to, for muftie and unwholfome Cafk.

That order be taken, that no Hogs, Dogs, or Cats, or tame Pigeons, or Conies bee fuffered to bee kept within any part of the City, or any Swine to bee, or ftray in the Streets or Lanes, but that fuch Swine bee impounded by the Beadle or any other Officer, and the Owner punifhed according to the Act of Com-mon-councell, and that the Dogs bee killed by the Dog-killers appointed for that purpofe.

Orders concerning loofe Perfons and idle Affemblies.

Beggers.

Orafmuch as nothing is more complained on, then the multitude of Rogues and wandering Beggers that fwarm in every place about the City, being a great caufe of the fpreading of the In-fection, and will not be avoided, notwithftanding any Order that hath been given to the contrary: It is there-fore now ordered, that fuch Conftables, and others whom this matter may any way concerne, doe take fpeciall care, that no wandering Begger be fuffered in the Streets of this City, in any fafhion or manner what-

Orders for health.

whatfoever upon pain of the penalty provided by t Law to be duely and feverely executed upon them.

Playes.

THat all Playes, Beare-batings, Games, Singing of Ballads, Buckler-play, or fuch like caufes o Affemblies of people, bee utterly prohibited, and the parties offending, feverely punifhed, by any Al-derman, or Juftice of the peace.

Tipling houfes.

THat diforderly Tipling in Tavernes Ale-houfes and Cellers, be feverely looked unto, as the com-mon finne of this time, and greateft occafion of dif-perfing the Plague: and where any fhall be found to offend, the penalty of the Statute to be laid upon them with all feverity.

And for the better execution of thefe Orders, as alfo for fuch other directions as fhall be needfull, it is agreed that the Juftices of the City and Counties ad-joyning doe meete together once in ten dayes either at the Seffions houfe without Newgate, or fome other convenient, place to conferre of things as fhall be need-full in this behalfe.

And every perfon neglecting the duty required, or willingly offending againft any Article or claufe con-tained in thefe Orders, he to be feverely punifhed by imprifonment, or otherwife, as by the law he ought.

God fave the King.

Plague orders issued by the Lord Mayor of London.

More violent entertainment was available too – bear-baiting, bull-baiting and cock-fighting. During the plague year of 1665, shops and taverns were also closed and fairs were banned. All sports were forbidden and everyone had to be indoors by nine o'clock in the evening.

Bakers were privileged freemen of the City of London. They were ordered to keep baking during the Great Plague or lose their privileges.

HERBAL REMEDIES

O ne major effect of the Great Plague was to turn public health and medical science into areas of interest and research. In May 1665 the College of Physicians was asked to provide remedies for plague sufferers. The college recommended the use of medicines containing herbs such as sage, rue, buttercup root, angelica root, snake-root and saffron infused in malaga.

People thought that tobacco and snuff gave protection against disease. The men who collected the bodies of plague victims often smoked pipes.

These herbs were believed to protect against plague.

A dead plague victim being dissected. The physicians are burning herbs over hot coals.

The Manner of Dissecting the PESTILENTIALL BODY.

The physician Nathaniel Hodges cared for plague victims. He tried to guard against infection by burning a 'disinfectant' over hot coals. In common with others at that time, he believed that disease was the result of 'nitrous spirit' that came from inside the earth.

rosemary

lavender

bay

Herbs were burned in pots like this one to keep plague away.

THE SILENT CITY

The winter of 1664-5 was bitterly cold. On 6 February 1665 Pepys wrote: "One of the coldest days, all say, they ever felt in England." In the following months the cold gradually gave way to hot, sultry weather, bringing swarms of flies to the rubbish-filled streets. By 24 May plague deaths were causing unease and Pepys wrote: "...news of the plague growing upon us in this town." By 7 June Pepys could record: "The hottest day that ever I felt in my life." On the same day he observed red crosses on the doors of houses in Drury Lane, London. By 29 June he was seeing wagons leaving the city as Londoners fled. His diary entry for 8 August describes the streets of London as: "...empty all the way."

Plague-infected houses were marked with a red cross about 30 cm. long and wide.

By mid-July 1665, 10,000 houses
stood empty in London. Over 200,000 people had fled.

PLAGUE ORDERS

Parish officials in London, known as constables, had instructions to oversee street-cleaning, rubbish disposal and the restrictions on public gatherings.

40,000 dogs were killed by appointed dog-killers. Pigs, dogs, cats and pigeons were not allowed on the streets.

Deaths had to be recorded, infected houses closed up and beggars arrested. Plague 'examiners' were appointed to report cases of sickness. Street cleaning was organised by 'scavengers'. 'Rakers' cleared away sewage and rotting rubbish and threw it into the river.

It was believed that bonfires 'cleaned' the air. Pepys wrote in early September 1665: "...saw fires burning in the street, as it is through the whole city, by the Lord Mayor's order..."

Bonfires were lit on street corners. 'Watchers' guarded infected houses day and night. Female 'searchers' carrying staffs examined the dead for signs of plague.

In 1625, public health regulations to deal with plague had been produced. The Lord Mayor of London issued similar orders in 1665.

Orders for Health.

confideration thought very expedient for preventing and avoiding of infection of Sicknefs (if it fhall fo pleafe Almighty God) that thefe Officers following be appointed, and thefe Orders hereafter duly obferved.

Examiners to be appointed in every Parifh.

First, It is thought requifite and fo ordered, that in every Parifh there be one, two, or more perfons of good fort and credit, chofen and appointed by the Alderman, his Deputy, and Common-Council of every Ward, by the name of Examiners, to continue in that Office the fpace of two Moneths at leaft: And if any fit Perfon fo appointed, fhall refufe to undertake the fame, the faid parties fo refufing, to be committed to Prifon until they fhall conform themfelves accordingly.

The Examiners Office.

That thefe Examiners be fworn by the Alderman, to enquire and learn from time to time what Houfes in every Parifh be vifited, and what perfons be fick, and of what Difeafes, as near as they can inform themfelves; and upon doubt in that cafe, to command reftraint of accefs, until it appear what the Difeafe fhall prove: And if they finde any perfon fick of the Infection, to give order to the Conftable that the Houfe be fhut up; and if the Conftable fhall be found remifs or negligent, to give prefent notice thereof to the Alderman of the Ward.

Watchmen.

That to every Infected Houfe there be appointed two Watchmen, one for the Day, and the other for the Night: And that thefe Watchmen have a fpecial care that no perfon goe in or out of fuch infected Houfes, whereof they have the Charge, upon pain of fevere punifhment. And the faid Watchmen to doe fuch further Offices as the fick Houfe fhall need and require: And if the Watchman be fent upon any bufinefs, to lock up the Houfe and take the Key with him: and the Watchman by day to attend until ten of the clock at night: and the Watchman by night until fix in the morning.

Searchers.

That there be a fpecial care, to appoint Women-Searchers in every Parifh, fuch as are of honeft reputation, and of the beft fort as can be got in this kind: And thefe to be fworn to make due fearch and true report, to the utmoft of their knowledge, whether the Perfons, whofe bodies they are appointed to Search, do die of the Infection, or of what other Difeafes, as near as they can. And that the Phyficians who fhall be appointed for cure and prevention of the Infection, do call before them the faid Searchers who are or fhall be appointed for the feveral Parifhes under their refpective Cares, to the end they may confider whether they are fitly qualified for that employment; and charge them

PHYSICIANS FLEE

There were few qualified doctors, or physicians as they were then called, in 1665. Many physicians fled from London during the Great Plague. Those who remained, like Nathaniel Hodges, wore a special hood when they attended plague victims. The 'beak' of the hood was stuffed with herbs and spices, which were thought to prevent the wearer from catching plague. There were no cures for plague so people resorted to wearing magic charms.

A B R A C A D A B R A
A B R A C A D A B R
A B R A C A D A B
A B R A C A D A
A B R A C A D
A B R A C A
A B R A C
A B R A
A B R
A B
A

Charms like this were sold by pedlars and worn as protection against plague.

The front of the hood covering the nose and mouth was filled with herbs and spices.

A popular charm was the word 'abracadabra' arranged in the shape of a triangle and worn round the neck. The Lord Mayor of London, Sir William Lawrence, worked courageously to help the suffering population during the Great Plague.

The inscription on this commemorative silver-gilt plague spoon reads: "...when died at London of the plague 68,596, of all diseases 97,306."

37

PLAGUE PITS

There were only three hospitals in London in 1665 – St. Thomas's, St. Bartholomew's and Bedlam, a hospital for the insane. Plague victims had to be nursed at home or sent to a 'pesthouse'. The City of London's pesthouse was near Old Street. There were three more in Westminster and one in Stepney. Bills of Mortality, listing the number of people who had died each week and the cause of death, were sold for one penny (1d). Deaths were reported by the 'searchers', who were paid fourpence (4d) for each body.

Graveyards were full so mass burials took place in plague pits. The site of the present-day Liverpool Street station was once a burial ground. Nathaniel Hodges wrote: "The burying places would not hold the dead, so they were thrown into large pits dug in waste ground, in heaps thirty or forty together."

"Bring out your dead!"

Corpses lay in the streets. Families of the dead were locked inside their houses for 40 days. Corpse-bearers took bodies to burial pits for one shilling (12d) a time. These plague pits had to be at least two metres deep. Burials took place at night.

Mortality figures for 1665:

MONTH	CHRISTENED	BURIED	PLAGUE
January	1,150	2,041	0
February	910	1,644	1
March	931	1,590	0
April	1,003	1,460	2
May	1,135	1,873	43
June	843	2,262	590
July	791	6,820	4,127
August	899	25,427	19,046
September	657	30,699	26,230
October	638	7,201	14,373
November	428	4,595	3,449
December	403	1,395	734

A plague bell was rung in the streets to announce the collection of corpses. A university student wrote to his tutor in July 1665: "There dye so many that the bell would hardly ever leave ringing and so they ring not at all."

FACT OR FICTION?

D aniel Defoe wrote stories about the Great Plague some years after it happened. One of his characters, a drunken piper, is thrown into a plague cart. Fortunately he wakes up before the cart reaches the burial pit. This is probably just a story but a stone statue of a piper and his dog, carved about 1680-90, has survived and can still be seen in a London museum.

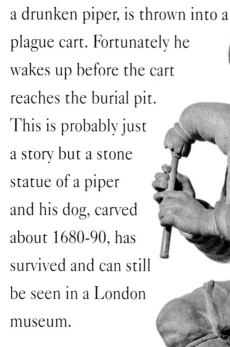

Boy playing bagpipes by Caius Gabriel Cibber (1630-1700). Carvings by this sculptor can also be seen in St. Paul's Cathedral and on the Monument to the Great Fire of London.

40

On 4 September 1665, Pepys describes in a letter the story of a child's escape from a plague-infected house. This famous painting of the incident by Frank Topham is from 1898.

Defoe also describes the experiences of families who were imprisoned in their homes. The watchman outside was sometimes attacked – even murdered: "...They blew up a watchman with gunpowder...the whole family that were able to stir got out at the windows one storey high..." This may also be just a story, as it was often the plague victims who were murdered by the people looking after them.

Rain came in September 1665. Plague deaths were averaging 1,000 a day. Corpses were rotting in the streets because the plague pits were full, but the worst was over. Fewer deaths were recorded after this time. People who had fled from London took plague to other parts of England. Most large towns were affected, including Southampton and Dover in the south, Ipswich and Yarmouth in the east, and Bristol and Gloucester in the west.

*The graves of plague victims can
be seen today outside Eyam.*

In the Midlands, Leicester
suffered badly and the village
of Eyam in Derbyshire
experienced a terrible tragedy
that is still remembered
today. Charles II returned to
London in February 1666. On
2 September 1666, the Great
Fire of London broke out. It
finally cleared London of the
Great Plague.

*Plague reached Eyam in a package of cloth
in September 1665. The 350 villagers unselfishly
decided to isolate themselves to stop the disease spreading
to other villages and towns. 260 inhabitants died.*

43

PREVENTING PLAGUE

B y the end of Charles II's reign, rickets had taken the place of plague as the most common disease. But lessons had been learned and the importance of medical science and the keeping of medical statistics were now recognised. Plague still recurs in some parts of the world. Most of the time it is kept under control but occasionally there are outbreaks.

European alert at airports as Indian plague spreads

By MARIANNE CURPHEY, NIGEL HAWKES AND EMMA WILKINS

HEALTH officials were meeting last night to consider Britain's response to the threat of pneumonic plague being carried in by visitors from India as other European countries announced precautions at airports.

Fear of the spread of the most infectious and most fatal form of the disease rose as Indian authorities confirmed that it had been carried from Surat, 160 miles north of ___ to the capital Delhi,

board who are ill". The Foreign Office has also warned holidaymakers going to Delhi to be "vigilant" and is recommending travellers to avoid Surat and the state of Gujarat. Tour operators, guided by Foreign Office advice, are still sending clients to India.

The Indian High Commission in London has be deluged with calls from w ried tourists, but emphasi that outbreaks of panic cau by news of the plague more widespread than

Menace of deadly old enemy

By NIGEL HAWKES
SCIENCE EDITOR

PLAGUE, known in the Middle Ages as the Black Death, has been a dangerous enemy of mankind from the earliest times.

The last widespread outbreak in Britain was the Great Plague of 1664-65; there was, however, a much smaller outbreak in Glasgow as recently as 1900.

In some areas of the world, including parts of China, India, and East Africa, plague is endemic. It remains under control most of the time, but is prone to sudden ___

Statistics gathered after the Great Plague by John Graunt, a member of the Royal Society:

Only 7% of Londoners reached the age of 70. Out of 100 births, 36 died before the age of 6 and only 1 reached the age of 76.

In 1994, newspaper headlines caused panic when pneumonic plague was claimed to have broken out in India. Air travellers were screened by doctors. Afterwards Indian doctors denied that the outbreak of illness was plague. Diseases like smallpox have been wiped out through the work of the World Health Organisation. Campaigns against other infectious diseases like tuberculosis, AIDS and hepatitis are ongoing.

GLOSSARY

ABRACADABRA *A word once thought to possess magical powers. The letters were used to shape a triangular charm worn during plague epidemics.*

astrologer *A person who relates the positions and movements of the planets, sun and moon to human lives.*

Bills of Mortality *Weekly bills listing the total number of deaths for the 130 parishes in and around the City of London.*

comet *A heavenly body with a trailing tail of gas, which moves around the sun.*

Danse Macabre *A dance of death performed in the 14th century by men dressed as skeletons.*

epidemic *Many cases of the same infectious disease occurring at the same time.*

examiners *Plague officials who reported all infected houses, which were then closed up and marked with a red cross.*

nitrous spirit *These substances in the air were believed to come from inside the earth and were thought of as 'bad air'. They could be caused by an earthquake.*

pedlar *A person who travels around selling small items.*

Pell-mell *A game introduced in 1660. The Mall in London follows the line of the original ground in St. James's Park.*

penny (1d) *The bronze old penny was used in Britain until 1971. 240d = one pound (£1). 12d = one shilling (1s).*

Royal Society *Charles II granted a Royal Charter to a group of scientists in August 1660. They became known as the Royal Society for the Improvement of Natural Knowledge by Experiment.*

scrofula *Once known as 'king's evil', this disease caused swollen neck glands and was thought to be cured by the touch of the king.*

searchers *Women appointed by the parish to find out the cause of death during plague epidemics.*

shilling (12d) *The old British silver shilling was replaced by the current 5p piece in 1971.*

watchers *Plague officials who stood guard outside the locked homes of plague victims and their families.*

World Health Organisation (WHO) *Part of the United Nations, with headquarters in Geneva, Switzerland.*

INDEX